Now We're Going to Have to Spray for Politicians

Recent Books by Pat Oliphant

Are We There Yet?

So That's Where They Came From!

Oliphant's Anthem

Reaffirm the Status Quo

Off to the Revolution

Waiting for the Other Shoe to Drop

Why Do I Feel Uneasy

Now We're Going to Have to Spray for Politicians

Pat Oliphant

**Andrews McMeel
Publishing**

Kansas City

00 01 02 03 BAH 10 9 8 7 6 5 4 3 2 1

ISBN: 0-7407-0614-4

Library of Congress Catalog Card Number: LC 00-103481

──────── **ATTENTION: SCHOOLS AND BUSINESSES** ────────

Andrews McMeel books are available at quantity discounts with bulk purchase for educational, business, or sales promotional use. For information, please write to: Special Sales Department, Andrews McMeel Publishing, 4520 Main Street, Kansas City, Missouri 64111.

February 23, 1999

March 15, 1999

March 17, 1999

THE PRESIDENT & STAFF
PONDER THE NEXT MOVE...

April 6, 1999

April 30, 1999

May 10, 1999

July 6, 1999

GUESS WHO GETS TO CARRY THE CARPETBAG.

August 10, 1999

August 17, 1999

56

August 25, 1999

58

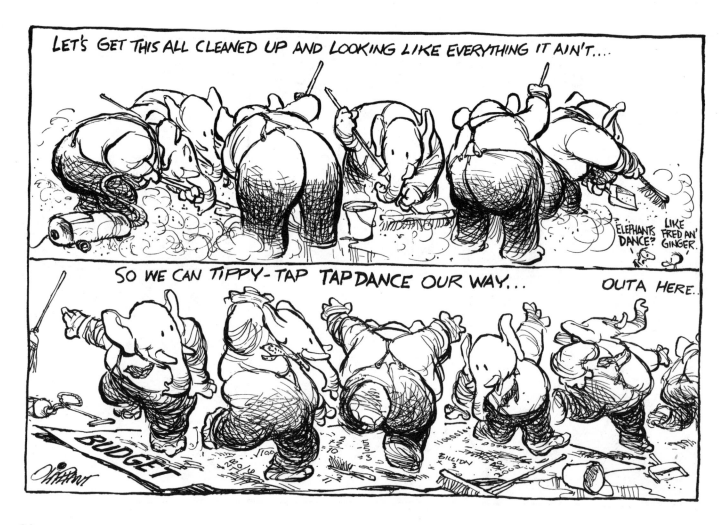

October 6, 1999

October 28, 1999

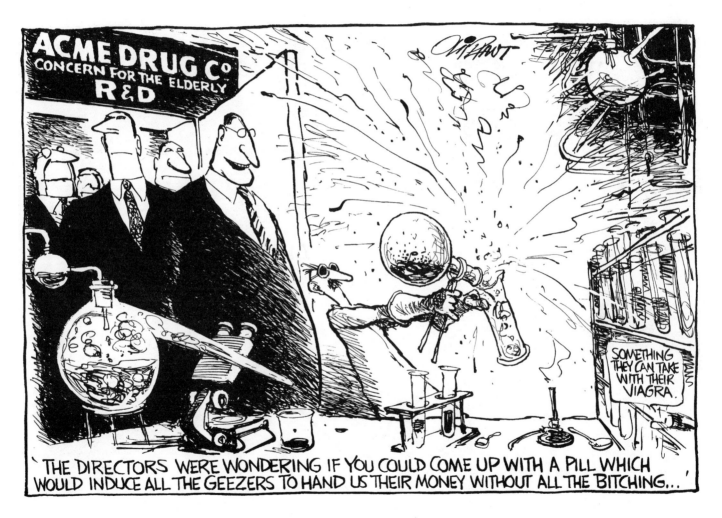

GOOD GRIEF, CHARLIE SCHULZ!

December 24, 1999

THE THREE WISEGUYS. (CONTINUED)

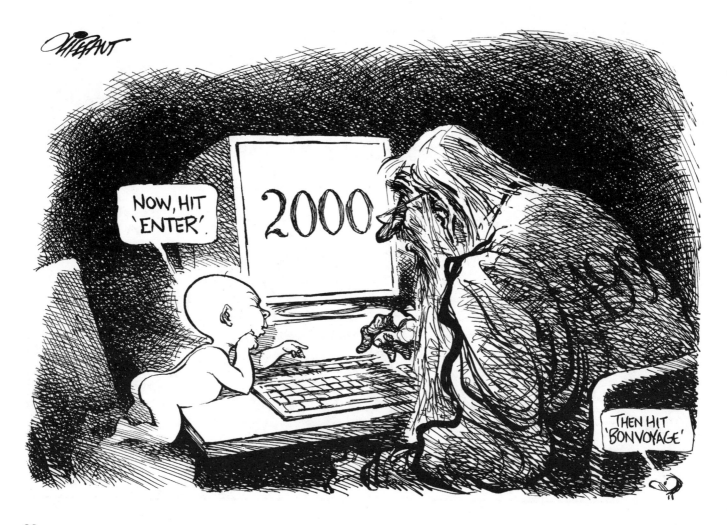

January 1, 2000

FELONY NUDE DANCING, A FIRST AMENDMENT ANOMALY.

May 18, 2000

May 24, 2000

June 7, 2000

133

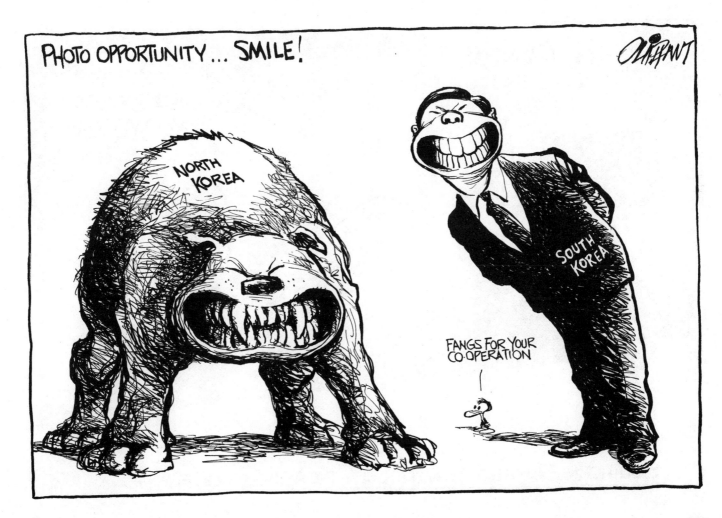

June 14, 2000

135

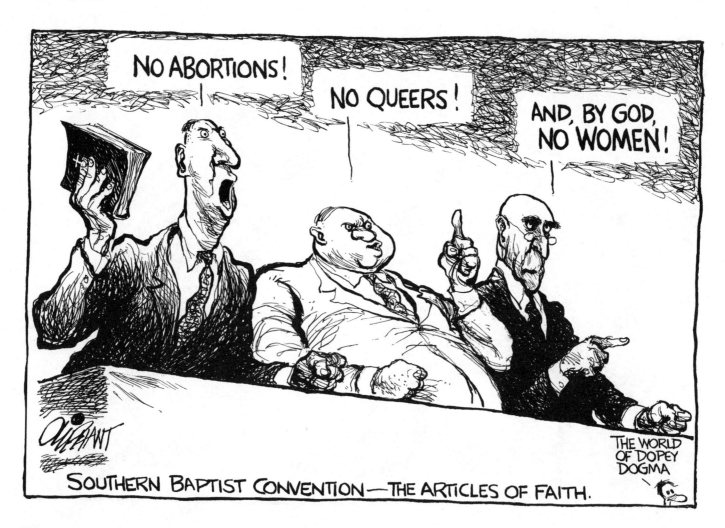

June 28, 2000

July 6, 2000

140

August 8, 2000

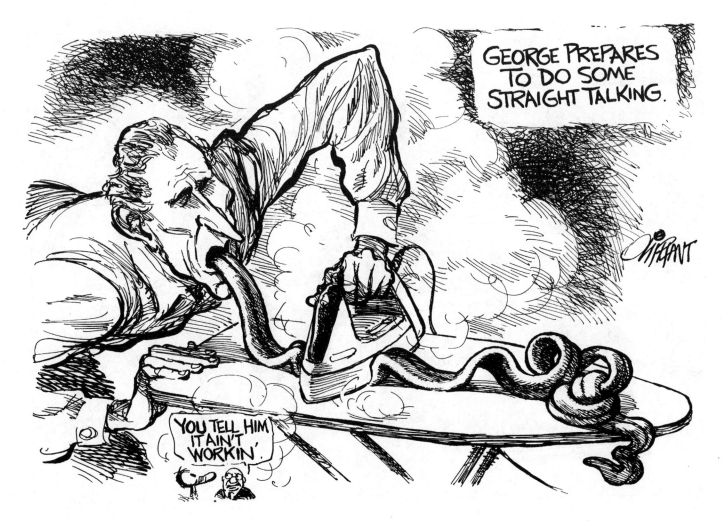

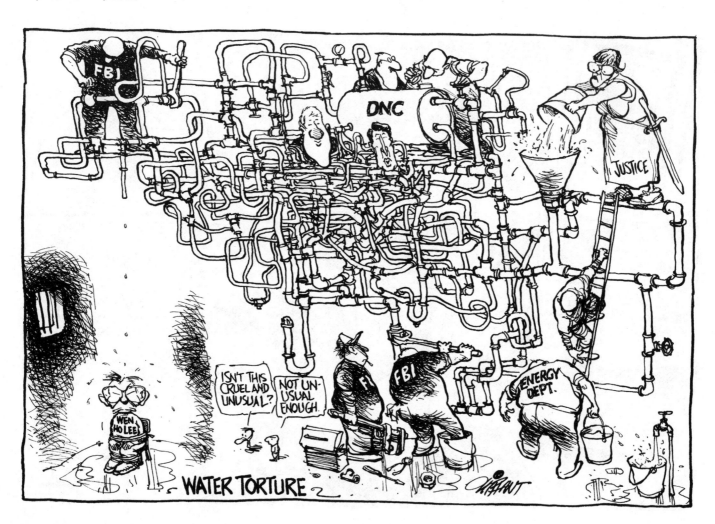

October 10, 2000

155